ITALIAN DRAWINGS

IN THE DEPARTMENT OF PRINTS AND DRAWINGS IN THE BRITISH MUSEUM

THE FOURTEENTH AND FIFTEENTH CENTURIES

ITALIAN DRAWINGS

IN THE DEPARTMENT OF PRINTS AND DRAWINGS IN THE BRITISH MUSEUM

—◆—

THE FOURTEENTH AND FIFTEENTH CENTURIES

—◆—

A. E. POPHAM AND PHILIP POUNCEY

Plates

PUBLISHED BY THE TRUSTEES OF THE BRITISH MUSEUM

LONDON

1950

Sold at
THE BRITISH MUSEUM *and by*
H.M. STATIONERY OFFICE, *York House, Kingsway, London, W.C.* 2,
BERNARD QUARITCH LTD., 11 *Grafton Street, London, W.* 1,
CAMBRIDGE UNIVERSITY PRESS, 200 *Euston Road, London, N.W.* 1,
and KEGAN PAUL, TRENCH, TRUBNER & Co.,
43 *Great Russell Street, London, W.C.* 1

PRINTED IN GREAT BRITAIN
AT THE UNIVERSITY PRESS, OXFORD
BY CHARLES BATEY, PRINTER TO THE UNIVERSITY

LIST OF PLATES

LIST OF PLATES

LIST OF PLATES

LIST OF PLATES

LIST OF PLATES

LIST OF PLATES

LIST OF PLATES

LIST OF PLATES

LIST OF PLATES

LIST OF PLATES

LIST OF PLATES

LIST OF PLATES

LIST OF PLATES

LIST OF PLATES

PLATE I

PROPHAETA. DAVID.

FRA ANGELICO

2

PLATE II

AFTER ALTICHIERO AND/OR AVANZO   1

ANONYMOUS   1 *verso*

PLATE III

SCHOOL OF FRA ANGELICO   3

PLATE IV

JACOPO DE' BARBARI 4

PLATE V

JACOPO DE' BARBARI   5

PLATE VI

GENTILE BELLINI

PLATE VII

GENTILE BELLINI

PLATE VIII

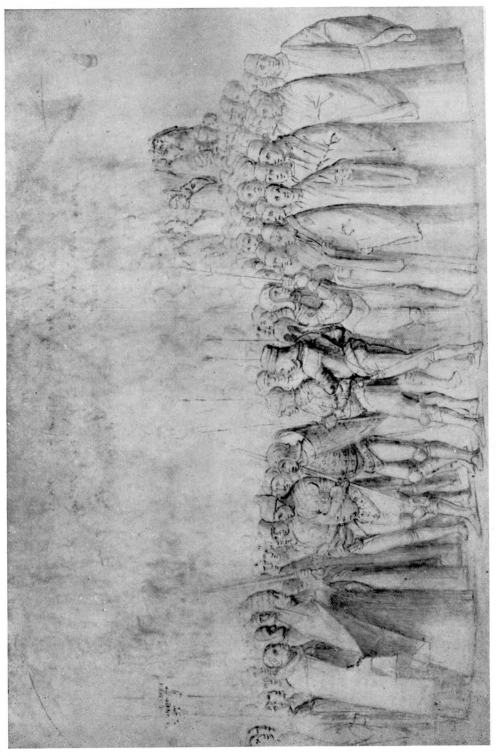

AFTER GENTILE BELLINI

PLATE IX

10

AFTER GENTILE BELLINI

PLATE X

ATTRIBUTED TO GIOVANNI
BELLINI

11

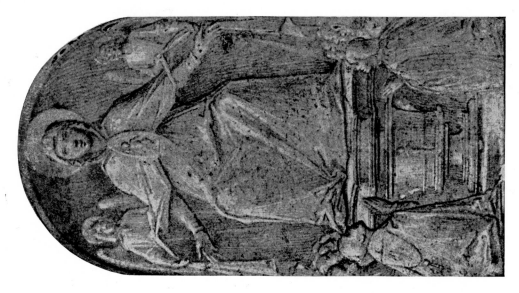

ATTRIBUTED TO LAZZARO BASTIANI

6

PLATE XI

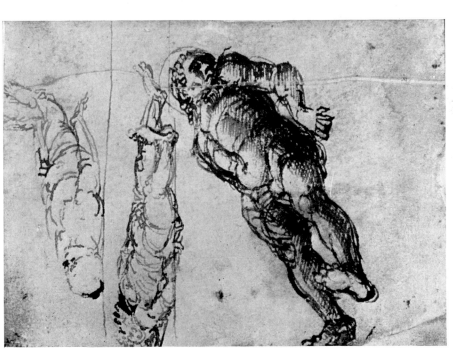

12 *verso*

12 *recto*

ATTRIBUTED TO GIOVANNI BELLINI

PLATE XII

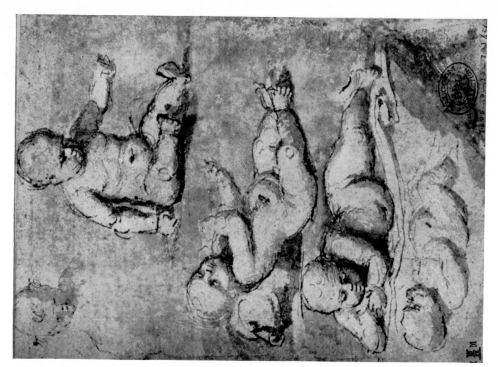

13 *verso*

13 *recto*

ATTRIBUTED TO GIOVANNI BELLINI

PLATE XIII

ATTRIBUTED TO GIOVANNI BELLINI

PLATE XIV

ATTRIBUTED TO GIOVANNI BELLINI

PLATE XV

ATTRIBUTED TO GIOVANNI BELLINI   16

PLATE XVI

18 *verso*

17

ATTRIBUTED TO GIOVANNI BELLINI

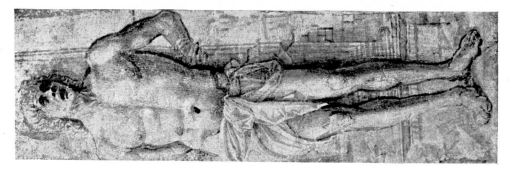

18 *recto*

PLATE XVII

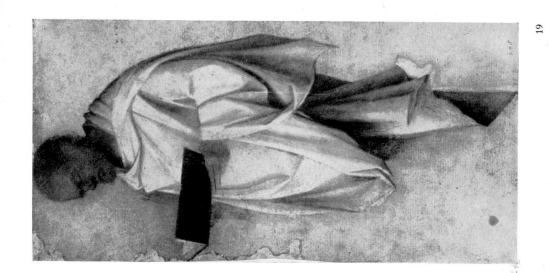

19

ATTRIBUTED TO GIOVANNI BELLINI

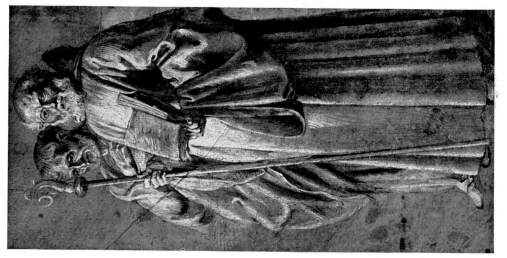

20

AFTER GIOVANNI BELLINI

PLATE XVIII

JACOPO BELLINI   21, fol. 66 *v*.

PLATE XIX

JACOPO BELLINI   21, fol. 67

PLATE XX

BOCCACCIO BOCCACCINO

PLATE XXI

FOLLOWER OF BOCCACCIO BOCCACCINO   23

PLATE XXII

SANDRO BOTTICELLI

PLATE XXIII

SANDRO BOTTICELLI 26

ATTRIBUTED TO BERNARDINO BUTINONE 31

PLATE XXIV

ATTRIBUTED TO RAFFAELLO BOTTICINI

PLATE XXV

ATTRIBUTED TO RAFFAELLO BOTTICINI   28

PLATE XXVI

ATTRIBUTED TO RAFFAELLO BOTTICINI

PLATE XXVII

AFTER SANDRO BOTTICELLI 27

PLATE XXVIII

PLATE XXIX

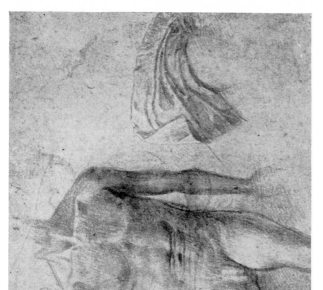

VITTORE CARPACCIO

PLATE XXX

VITTORE CARPACCIO

PLATE XXXI

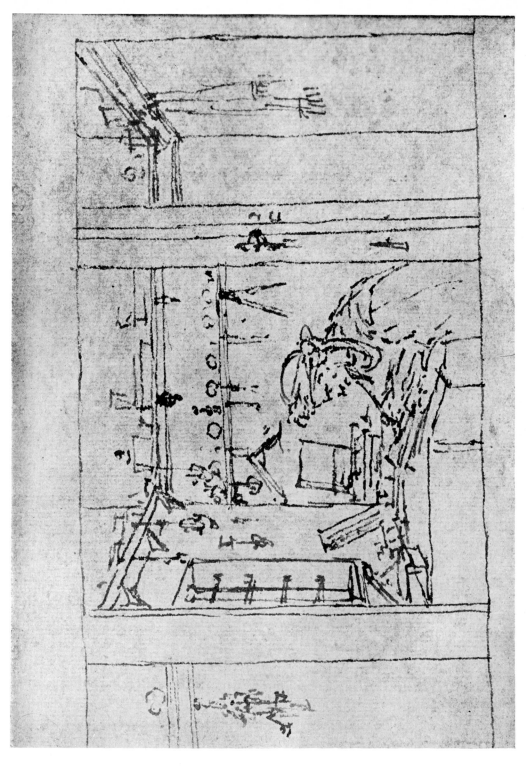

VITTORE CARPACCIO

PLATE XXXII

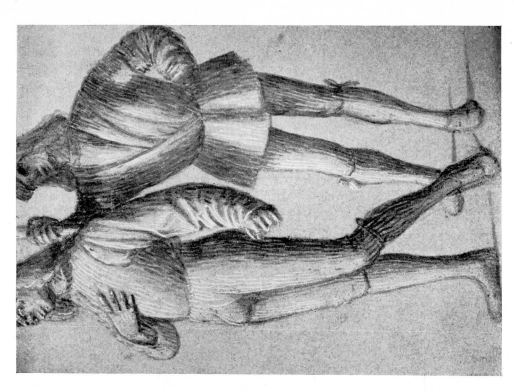

VITTORE CARPACCIO

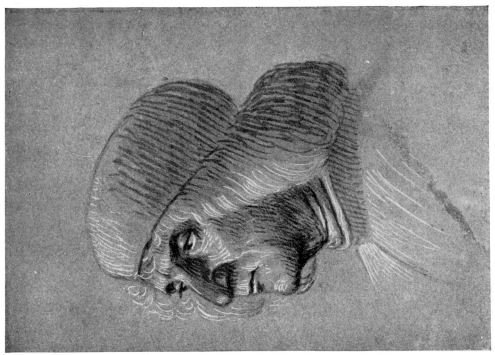

PLATE XXXIII

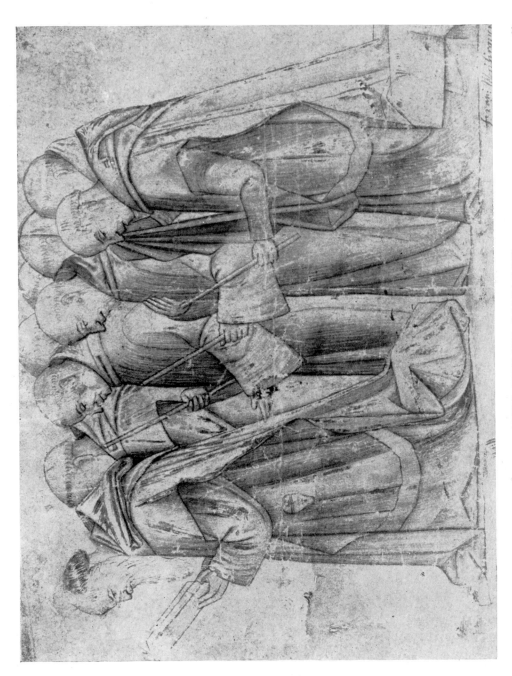

AFTER VITTORE CARPACCIO

PLATE XXXIV

34

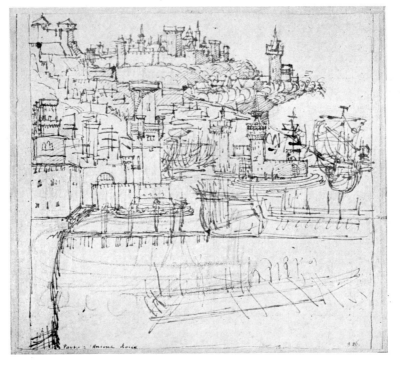

VITTORE CARPACCIO   33

PLATE XXXV

VITTORE CARPACCIO 37

PLATE XXXVI

GIOVANNI BATTISTA CIMA

PLATE XXXVII

GIOVANNI BATTISTA CIMA

PLATE XXXVIII

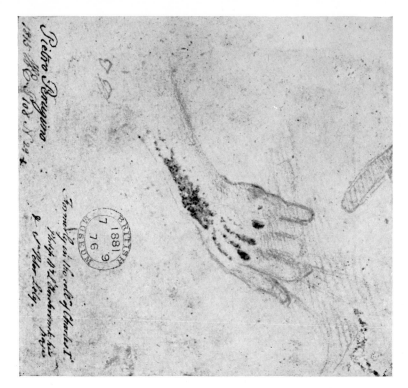

LORENZO COSTA

PLATE XXXIX

44

ATTRIBUTED TO LORENZO COSTA

PLATE XL

ATTRIBUTED TO FRANCESCO DEL COSSA   42

PLATE XLI

LORENZO DI CREDI

PLATE XLII

49

LORENZO DI CREDI

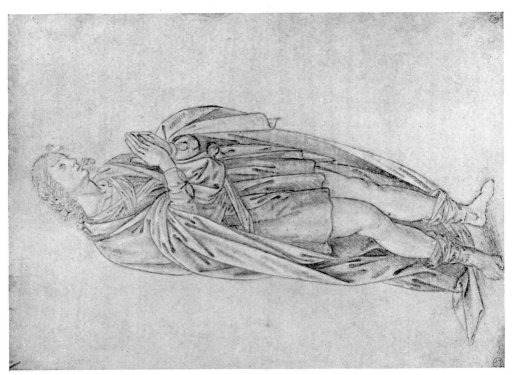

54

AFTER LORENZO DI CREDI

PLATE XLIII

50

51

LORENZO DI CREDI

PLATE XLIV

LORENZO DI CREDI 47

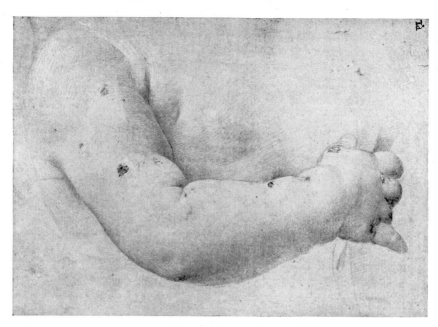

LORENZO DI CREDI 48

PLATE XLV

52 *recto*

ATTRIBUTED TO LORENZO DI CREDI 52 *verso*

PLATE XLVI

STUDIO OF LORENZO DI CREDI

PLATE XLVII

LORENZO DI CREDI   46

PLATE XLVIII

FRANCESCO DI GIORGIO   55, fol. 2

PLATE XLIX

FRANCESCO DI GIORGIO   55, fol. 32

PLATE L

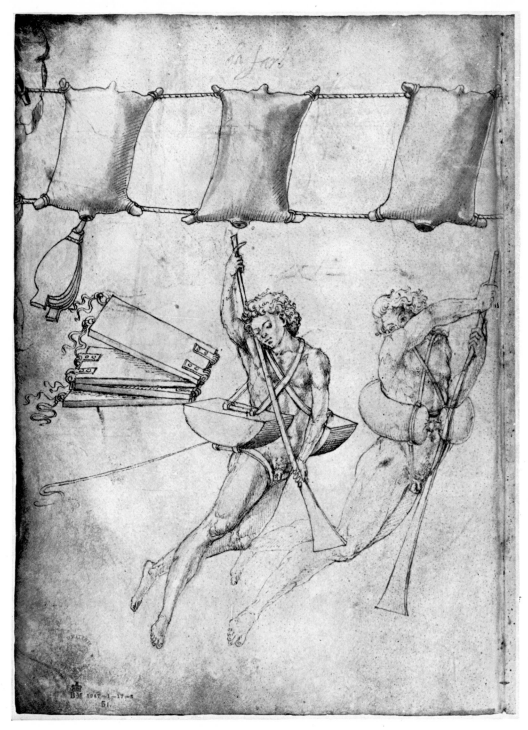

FRANCESCO DI GIORGIO   55, fol. 49 *v*.

PLATE LI

FRANCESCO DI GIORGIO   55, fol. 55 *v*.

PLATE LII

FRANCESCO DI GIORGIO   55, fol. *b.*

PLATE LIII

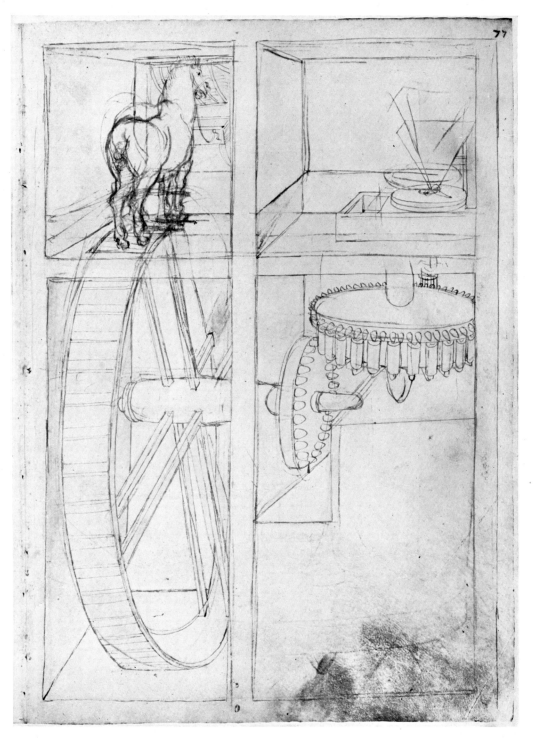

FRANCESCO DI GIORGIO · 55, fol. 77

PLATE LIV

ATTRIBUTED TO FRANCESCO DI SIMONE

PLATE LV

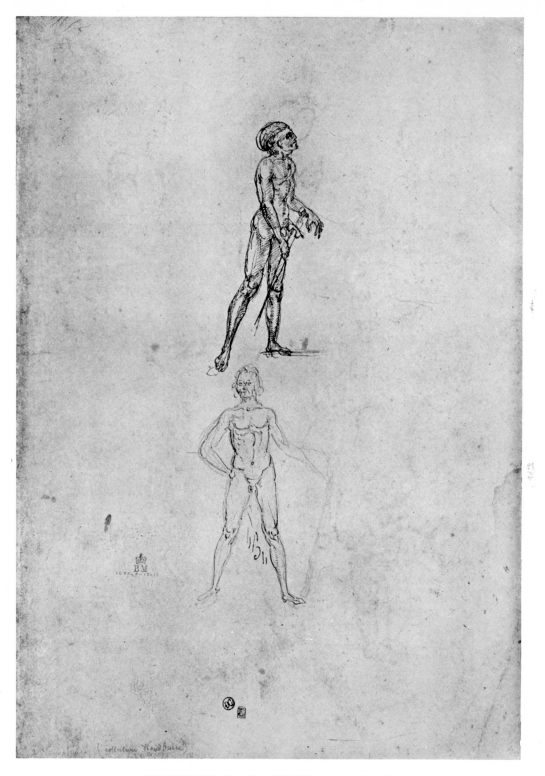

ATTRIBUTED TO FRANCESCO DI SIMONE

PLATE LVI

ATTRIBUTED TO FRANCESCO DI SIMONE 57 *recto*

PLATE LVII

ATTRIBUTED TO FRANCESCO DI SIMONE

57 *verso*

PLATE LVIII

FRANCESCO FRANCIA 58

PLATE LIX

ATTRIBUTED TO BERNARDINO FUNGAI

59

PLATE LX

RAFFAELLINO DEL GARBO

PLATE LXI

RAFFAELLINO DEL GARBO

PLATE LXII

RAFFAELLINO DEL GARBO

PLATE LXIII

63 recto

RAFFAELLINO DEL GARBO   *63 verso*

PLATE LXIV

61

RAFFAELLINO DEL GARBO

62

PLATE LXV

RAFFAELLINO DEL GARBO   60

PLATE LXVI

RAFFAELLINO DEL GARBO 68

PLATE LXVII

DOMENICO GHIRLANDAIO   71

PLATE LXVIII

DOMENICO GHIRLANDAIO

PLATE LXIX

DOMENICO GHIRLANDAIO

PLATE LXX

DOMENICO GHIRLANDAIO

PLATE LXXI

DOMENICO GHIRLANDAIO

PLATE LXXII

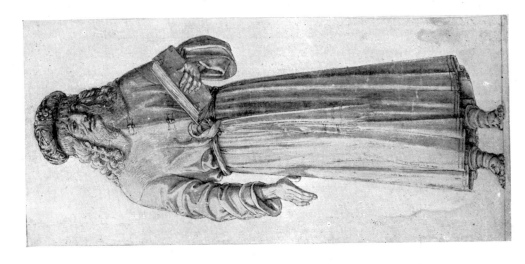

GIROLAMO DI BENVENUTO

PLATE LXXIII

77

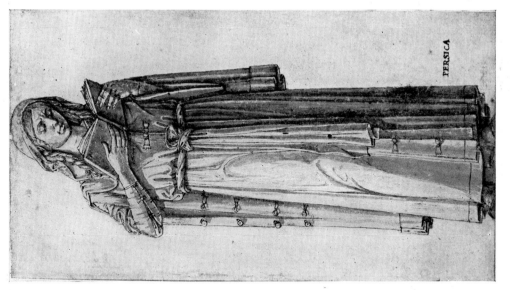

76

GIROLAMO DI BENVENUTO

PLATE LXXIV

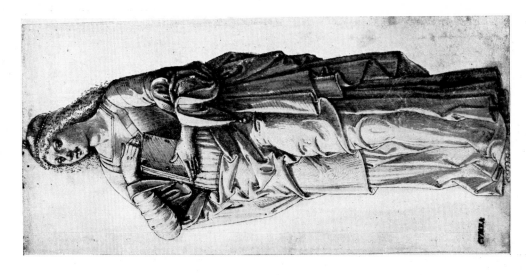

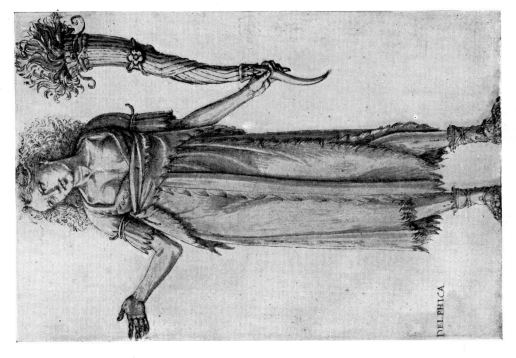

79

GIROLAMO DI BENVENUTO

78

PLATE LXXV

81

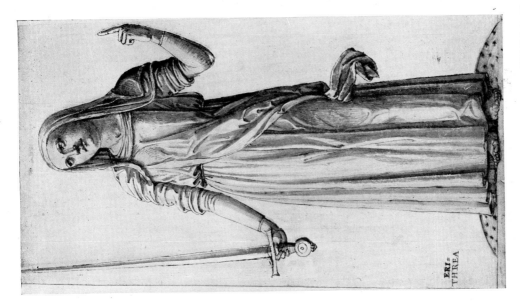

80

GIROLAMO DI BENVENUTO

PLATE LXXVI

83

SAMIA

CVMANA

82

GIROLAMO DI BENVENUTO

PLATE LXXVII

85

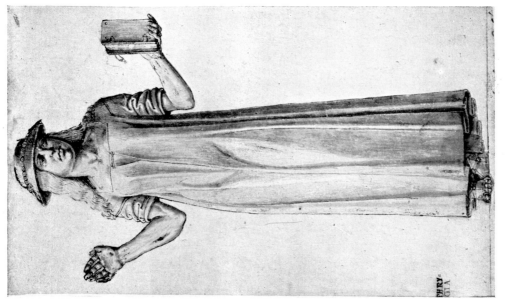

84

GIROLAMO DI BENVENUTO

PLATE LXXVIII

PLATE LXXIX

BENOZZO GOZZOLI

PLATE LXXX

SCHOOL OF BENOZZO GOZZOLI   91 *recto*

PLATE LXXXI

SCHOOL OF BENOZZO GOZZOLI   91 *verso*

PLATE LXXXII

BENOZZO GOZZOLI · · 87 *recto*

PLATE LXXXIII

BENOZZO GOZZOLI   87 *verso*

PLATE LXXXIV

BENOZZO GOZZOLI

PLATE LXXXV

SCHOOL OF BENOZZO GOZZOLI   93

PLATE LXXXVI

PLATE LXXXVII

SCHOOL OF BENOZZO GOZZOLI

PLATE LXXXVIII

LEONARDO DA VINCI

PLATE LXXXIX

LEONARDO DA VINCI

PLATE XC

LEONARDO DA VINCI

PLATE XCI

LEONARDO DA VINCI 98 *verso*

PLATE XCII

LEONARDO DA VINCI

99 recto

PLATE XCIII

LEONARDO DA VINCI   *99 verso*

PLATE XCIV

LEONARDO DA VINCI   100 *recto*

PLATE XCV

LEONARDO DA VINCI

100 verso

PLATE XCVI

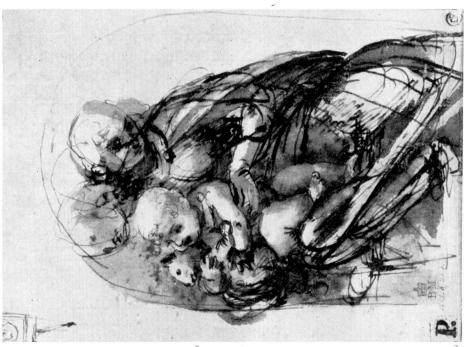

97 *verso*

LEONARDO DA VINCI

97 *recto*

PLATE XCVII

102

LEONARDO DA VINCI

103

PLATE XCVIII

LEONARDO DA VINCI 101

PLATE XCIX

LEONARDO DA VINCI   104

PLATE C

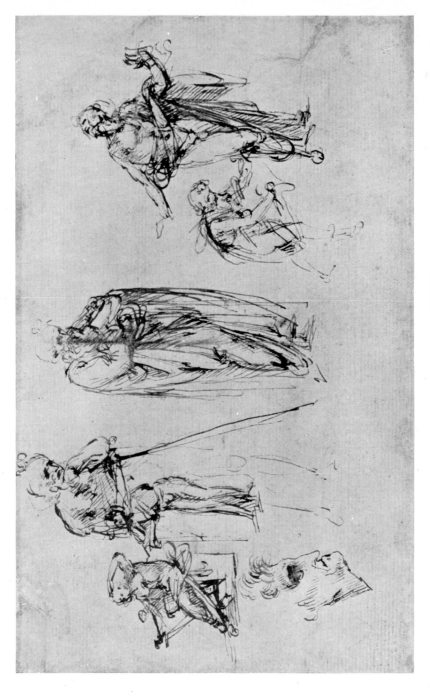

LEONARDO DA VINCI

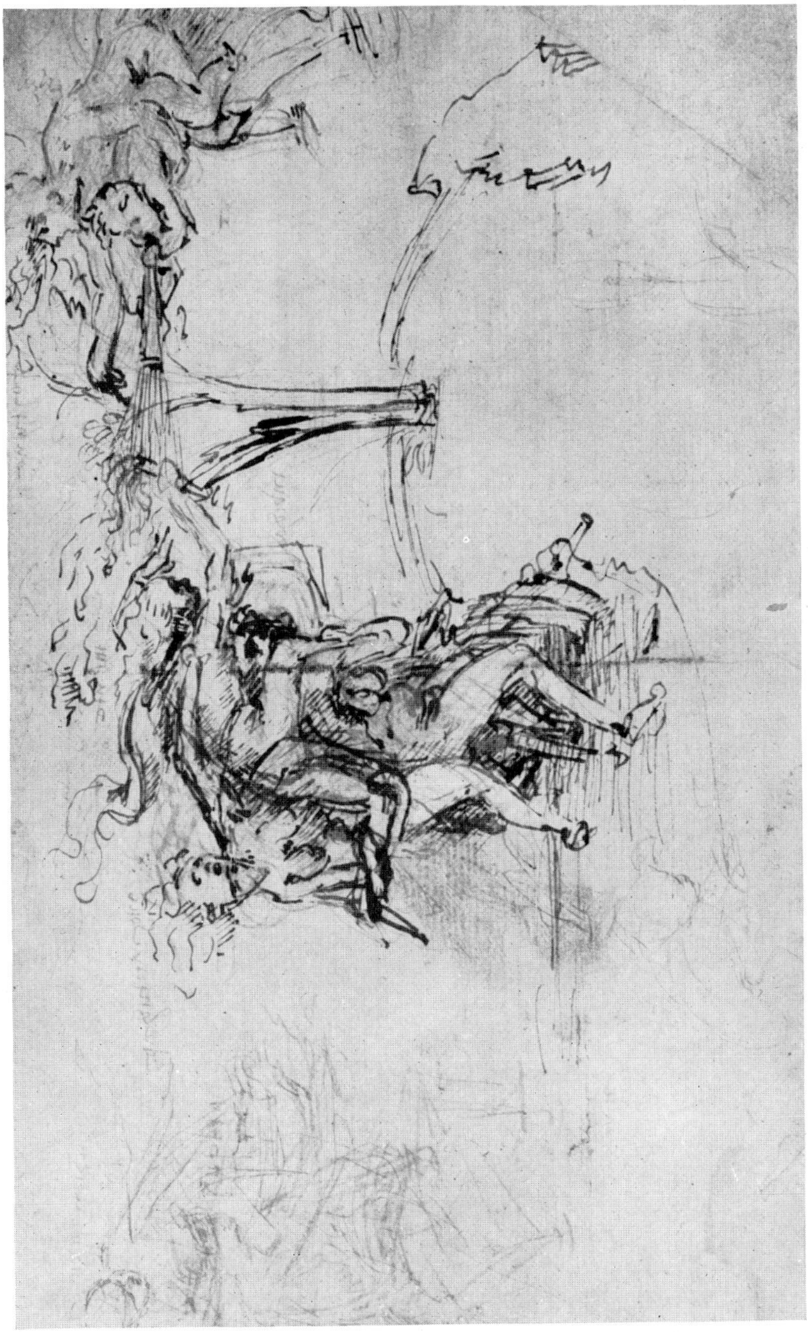

PLATE CI

LEONARDO DA VINCI

PLATE CII

LEONARDO DA VINCI

PLATE CIII

109 *verso*

LEONARDO DA VINCI

109 *recto*

PLATE CIV

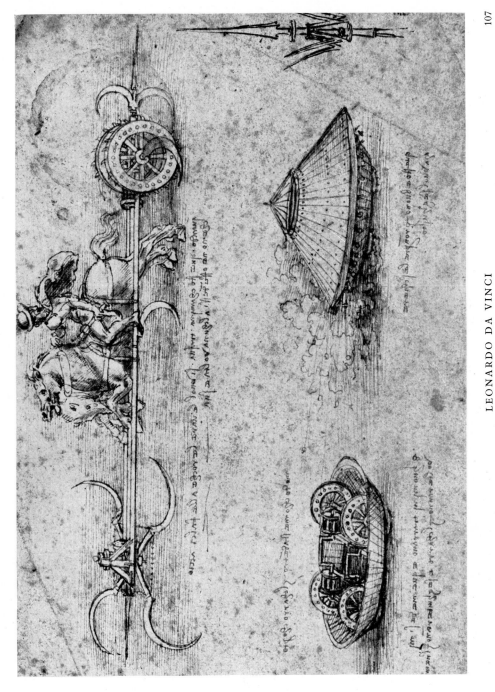

PLATE CV

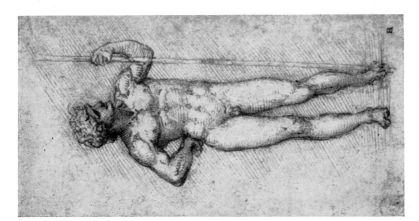

110

LEONARDO DA VINCI

111

PLATE CVI

LEONARDO DA VINCI

108 *recto*

PLATE CVII

108 *verso*

113   LEONARDO DA VINCI   114

PLATE CVIII

LEONARDO DA VINCI

PLATE CIX

AFTER LEONARDO DA VINCI   115

PLATE CX

122

AFTER LEONARDO DA VINCI

119

PLATE CXI

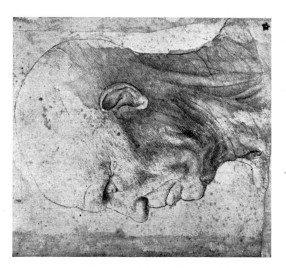

AFTER LEONARDO DA VINCI

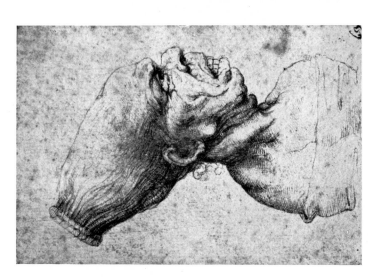

121

PLATE CXII

126

FOLLOWER OF LEONARDO DA VINCI

AFTER LEONARDO DA VINCI 117

PLATE CXIII

123

FOLLOWERS OF LEONARDO DA VINCI

124

PLATE CXIV

FOLLOWER OF LEONARDO DA VINCI

PLATE CXV

FOLLOWER OF LEONARDO DA VINCI

PLATE CXVI

AFTER LEONARDO DA VINCI

PLATE CXVII

FOLLOWER OF LEONARDO DA VINCI

PLATE CXVIII

LIBERALE DA VERONA

PLATE CXIX

LIBERALE DA VERONA   130

PLATE CXX

FILIPPINO LIPPI

PLATE CXXI

FILIPPINO LIPPI

133

PLATE CXXII

FILIPPINO LIPPI

134

PLATE CXXIII

FILIPPINO LIPPI

135

PLATE CXXIV

FILIPPINO LIPPI

136 *recto*

PLATE CXXV

FILIPPINO LIPPI   136 *verso*

PLATE CXXVI

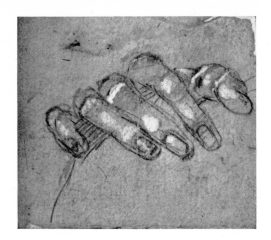

139

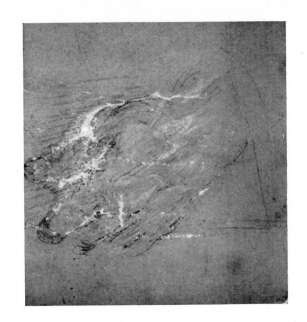

140

FILIPPINO LIPPI   137

PLATE CXXVII

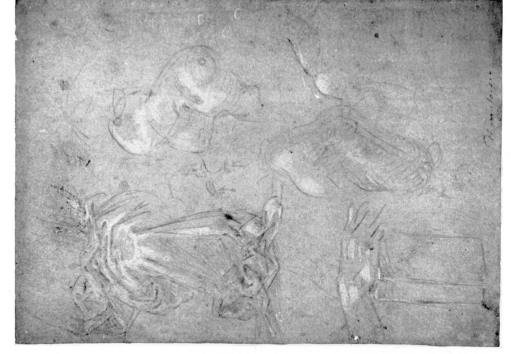

138 *recto*

FILIPPINO LIPPI

132

PLATE CXXVIII

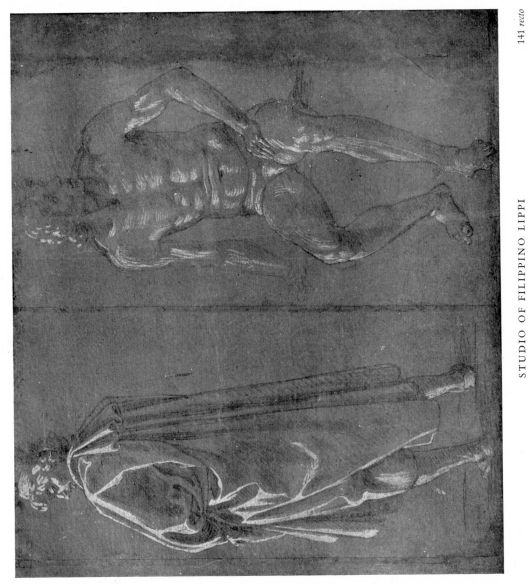

STUDIO OF FILIPPINO LIPPI

PLATE CXXIX

STUDIO OF FILIPPINO LIPPI

PLATE CXXX

PLATE CXXXI

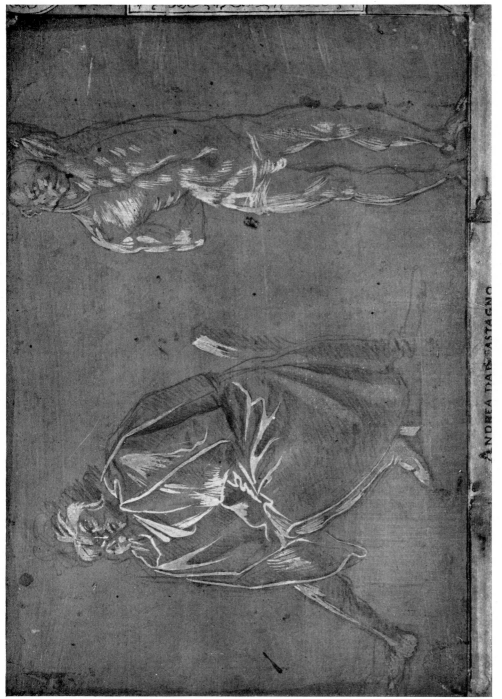

142 *verso*

ANDREA DAL CASTAGNO

STUDIO OF FILIPPINO LIPPI

PLATE CXXXII

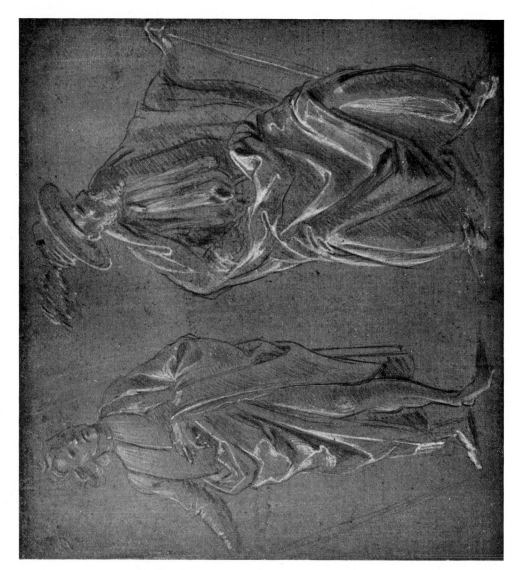

STUDIO OF FILIPPINO LIPPI

PLATE CXXXIII

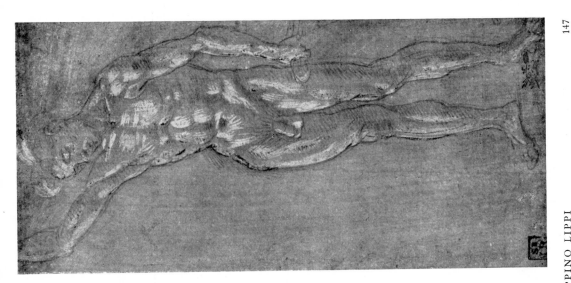

147

146

PLATE CXXXIV

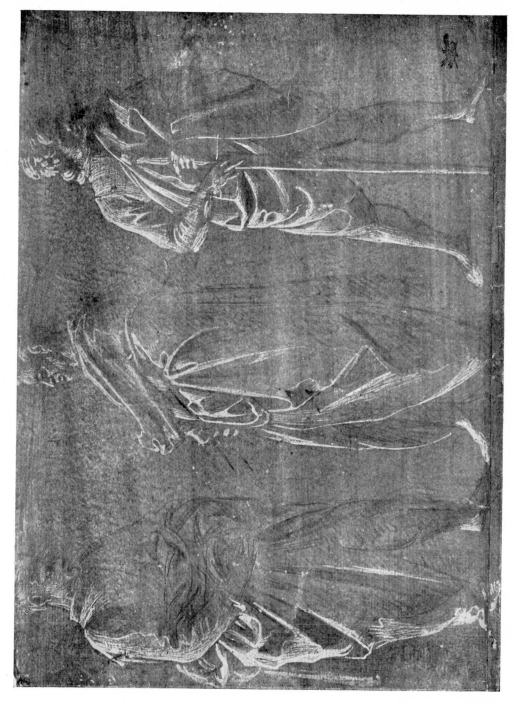

144 *recto*

STUDIO OF FILIPPINO LIPPI

PLATE CXXXV

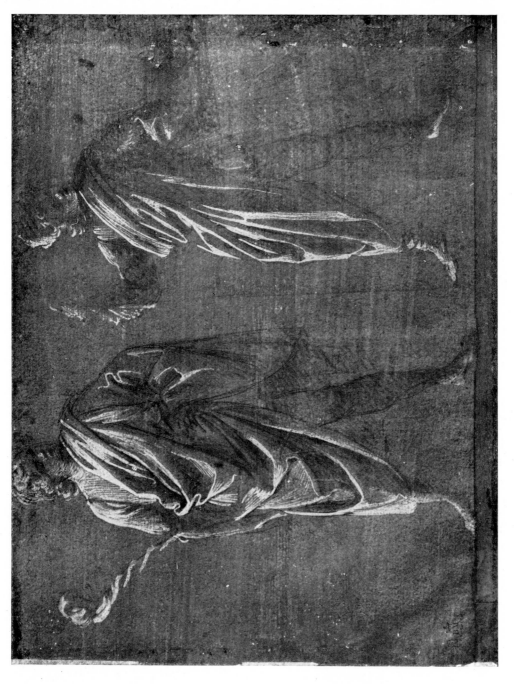

STUDIO OF FILIPPINO LIPPI

PLATE CXXXVI

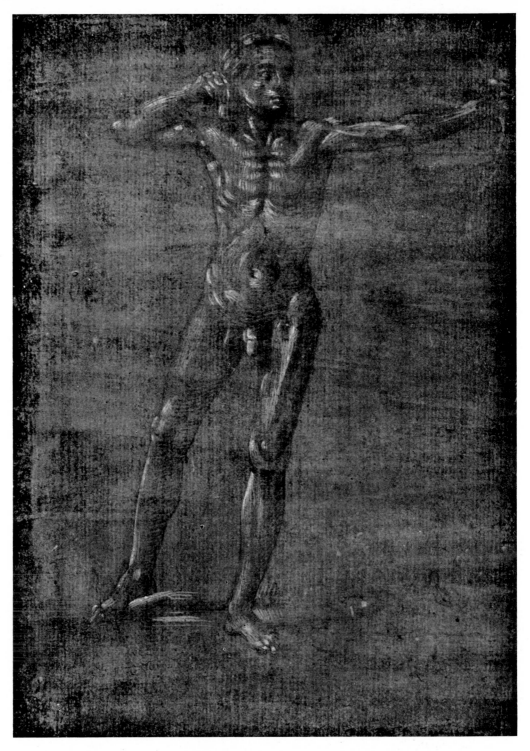

STUDIO OF FILIPPINO LIPPI

PLATE CXXXVII

STUDIO OF FILIPPINO LIPPI   148 *recto*

PLATE CXXXVIII

FILIPPO LIPPI 150 *recto*

PLATE CXXXIX

FILIPPO LIPPI   150 *verso*

PLATE CXL

FILIPPO LIPPI

149

PLATE CXLI

STUDIO OF FILIPPO LIPPI   152

PLATE CXLII

AFTER FILIPPO LIPPI 151 *recto*

ATTRIBUTED TO GIANFRANCESCO DE' MAINERI 154

PLATE CXLIII

BASTIANO DA S. GIMIGANO PITT:-

ATTRIBUTED TO BASTIANO MAINARDI 153

PLATE CXLIV

ANDREA MANTEGNA

PLATE CXLV

ANDREA MANTEGNA

PLATE CXLVI

ANDREA MANTEGNA

PLATE CXLVII

157

PLATE CXLVIII

ANDREA MANTEGNA

PLATE CXLIX

SCHOOL OF ANDREA MANTEGNA

162

PLATE CL

SCHOOL OF ANDREA MANTEGNA

PLATE CLI

SCHOOL OF ANDREA MANTEGNA 164

PLATE CLII

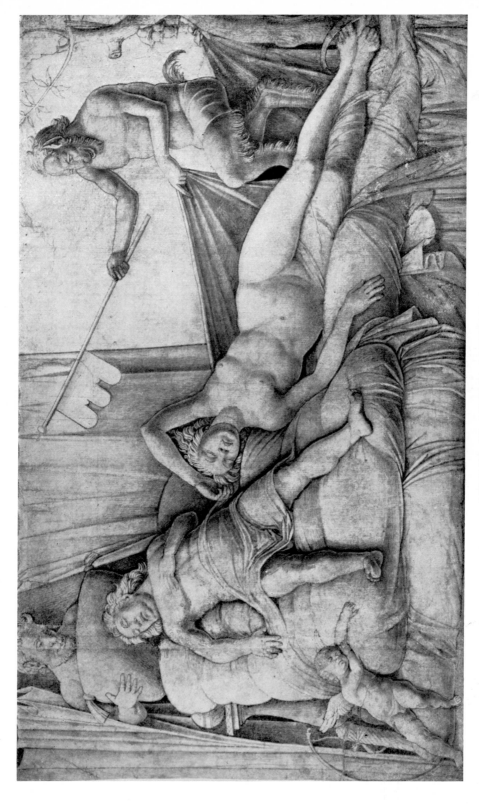

PLATE CLIII

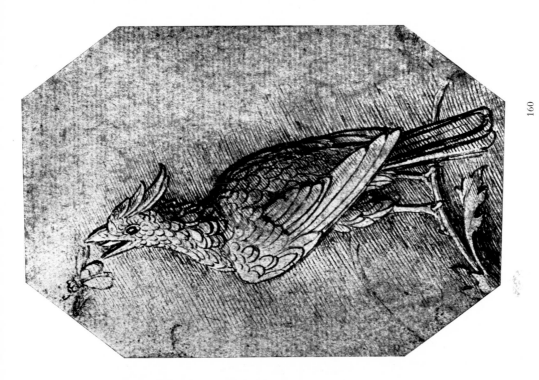

160

ANDREA MANTEGNA

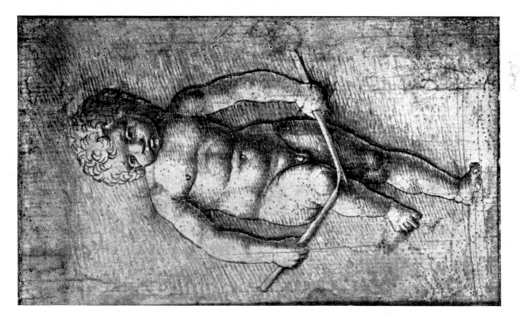

161 *verso* (a)

SCHOOL OF ANDREA MANTEGNA

PLATE CLIV

AFTER ANDREA MANTEGNA

PLATE CLV

169

AFTER ANDREA MANTEGNA

167

PLATE CLVI

AFTER ANDREA MANTEGNA

PLATE CLVII

MARIOTTO DI NARDO

170

PLATE CLVIII

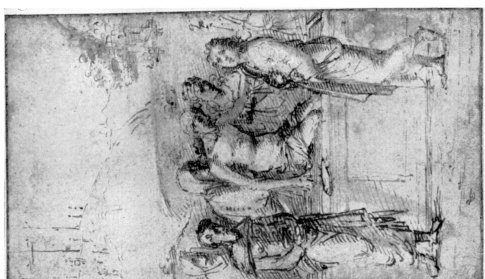

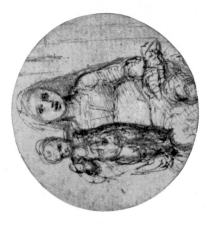

173

171

172

FRANCESCO MARMITTA

PLATE CLIX

FRANCESCO MARMITTA

PLATE CLX

AFTER FRANCESCO MARMITTA

PLATE CLXI

BARTOLOMEO MONTAGNA 176

PLATE CLXII

PLATE CLXIII

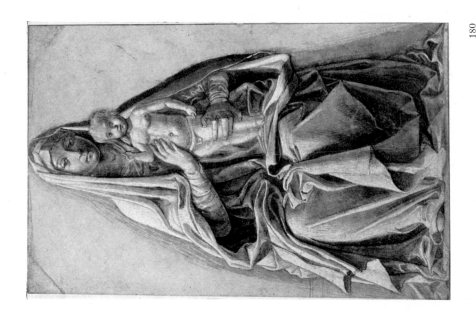

180

FOLLOWER OF BARTOLOMEO MONTAGNA

179

AFTER BARTOLOMEO MONTAGNA

PLATE CLXIV

182

181

ATTRIBUTED TO NICOLETTO DA MODENA

PLATE CLXV

183 *recto*

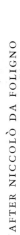

AFTER NICCOLÒ DA FOLIGNO

183 *verso*

PLATE CLXVI

MARCO PALMEZZANO

PLATE CLXVII

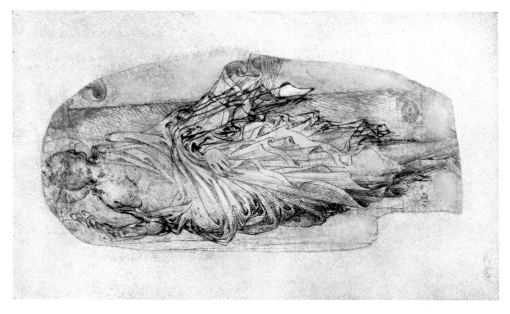

PARRI SPINELLI

186 *recto*

PLATE CLXVIII

BERNARDO PARENTINO

PLATE CLXIX

PIETRO PERUGINO
187 *recto*

PLATE CLXX

PIETRO PERUGINO

PLATE CLXXI

PIETRO PERUGINO   189

PLATE CLXXII

PIETRO PERUGINO

190

PLATE CLXXIII

PIETRO PERUGINO   191

PLATE CLXXIV

ASSISTANT OF PIETRO PERUGINO

PLATE CLXXV

SCHOOL OF PIETRO PERUGINO

209

PLATE CLXXVI

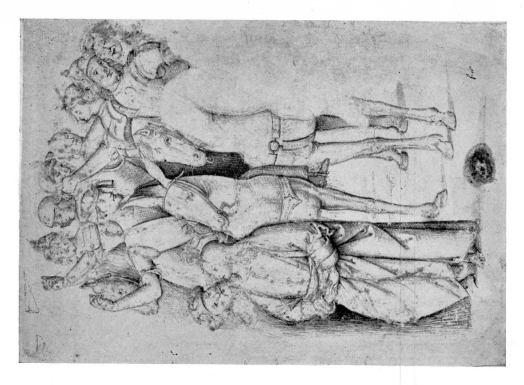

195

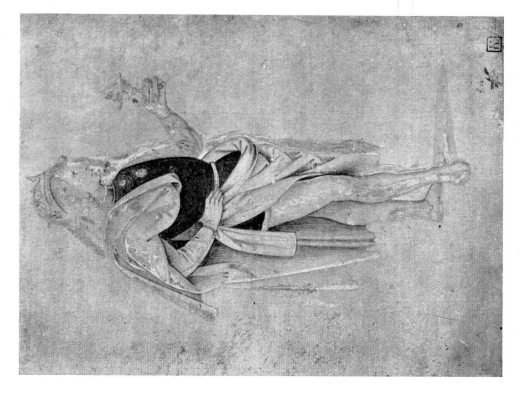

194

AFTER PIETRO PERUGINO

PLATE CLXXVII

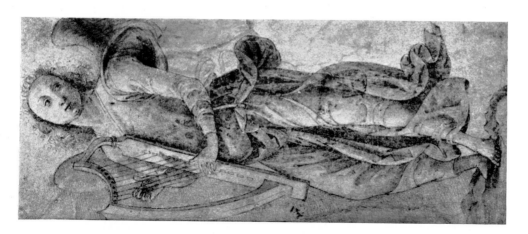

198

AFTER PIETRO PERUGINO

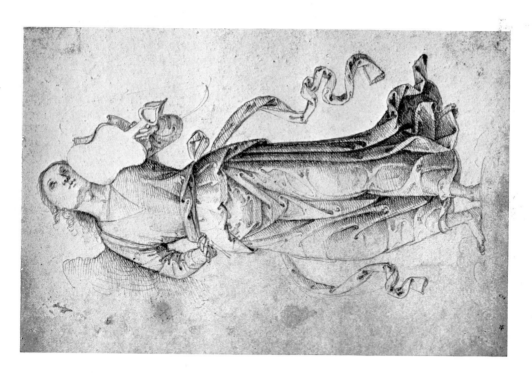

197

PLATE CLXXVIII

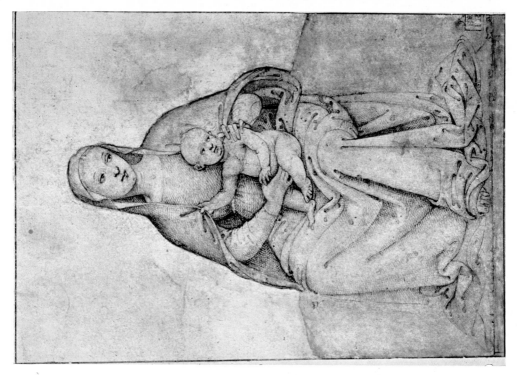

SCHOOL OF PIETRO PERUGINO

PLATE CLXXIX

PLATE CLXXX

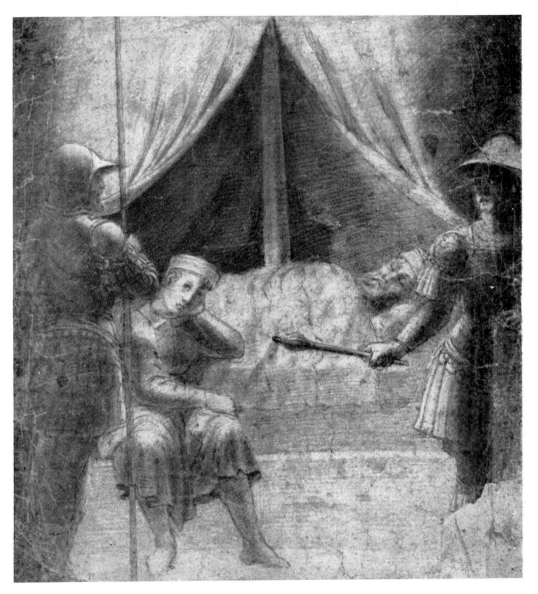

AFTER PIERO DELLA FRANCESCA

PLATE CLXXXI

ATTRIBUTED TO PIERO DI COSIMO

PLATE CLXXXII

212

PLATE CLXXXIII

214

BERNARDINO PINTORICCHIO

PLATE CLXXXIV

AFTER BERNARDINO PINTORICCHIO

PLATE CLXXXV

ATTRIBUTED TO BERNARDINO   215
PINTORICCHIO

AFTER BERNARDINO PINTORICCHIO (?)   218

PLATE CLXXXVI

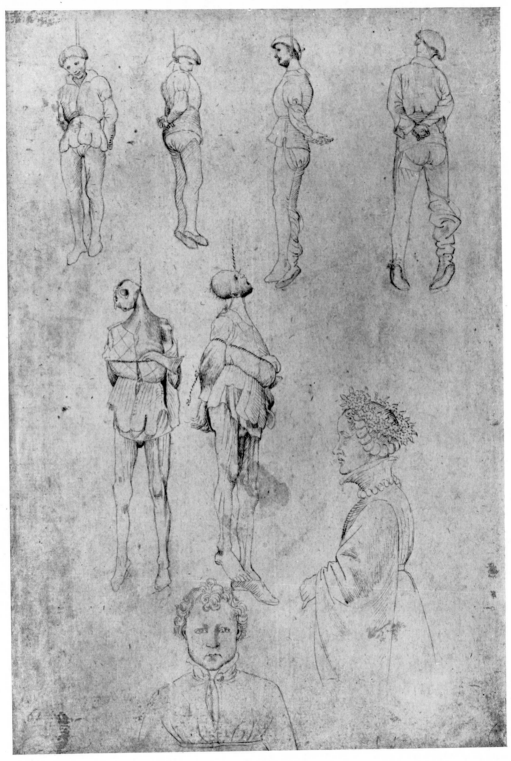

ANTONIO PISANELLO

PLATE CLXXXVII

221 recto

ANTONIO PISANELLO

221 verso

PLATE CLXXXVIII

ANTONIO PISANELLO

PLATE CLXXXIX

ANTONIO PISANELLO *222 verso*

PLATE CXC

219

ANTONIO PISANELLO

PLATE CXCI

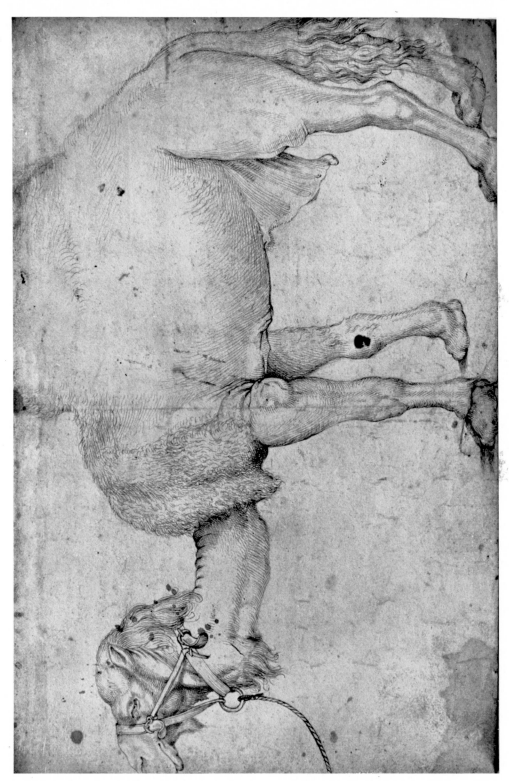

AFTER ANTONIO PISANELLO

PLATE CXCII

224

ANTONIO DEL POLLAIUOLO

PLATE CXCIII

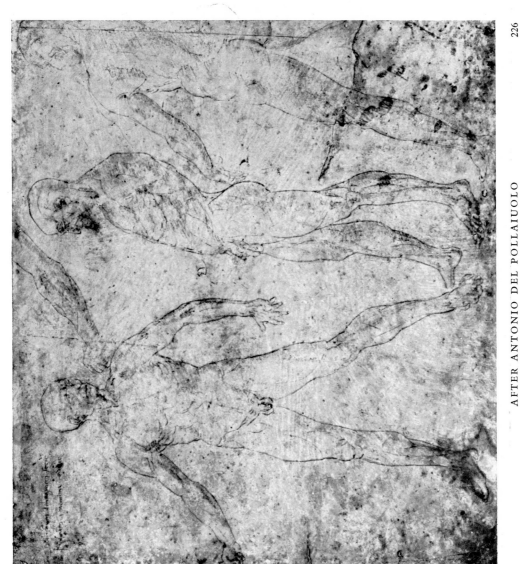

AFTER ANTONIO DEL POLLAIUOLO

PLATE CXCIV

ANTONIO DEL POLLAIUOLO

PLATE CXCV

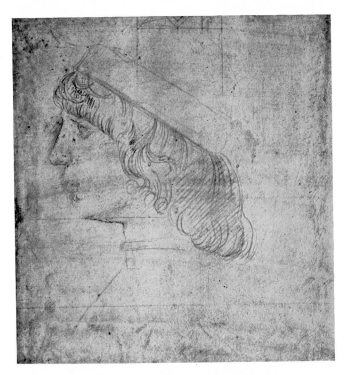

ATTRIBUTED TO AMBROGIO DE PREDIS   227

ANTONIO DEL POLLAIUOLO   225 *verso*

PLATE CXCVI

ATTRIBUTED TO ERCOLE DE' ROBERTI   228

AFTER ERCOLE DE' ROBERTI   230

PLATE CXCVII

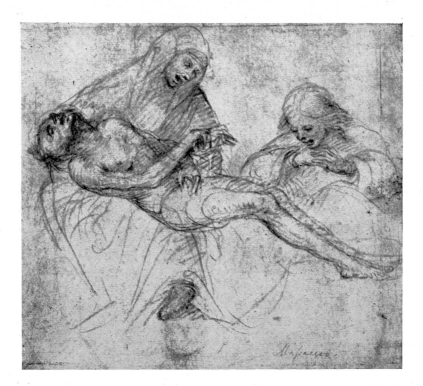

229 recto

ATTRIBUTED TO ERCOLE DE' ROBERTI   *229 verso*

PLATE CXCVIII

COSIMO ROSSELLI 231

ATTRIBUTED TO JACOPO DEL SELLAIO 233

PLATE CXCIX

AFTER ANTONIO ROSSELLINO

232

PLATE CC

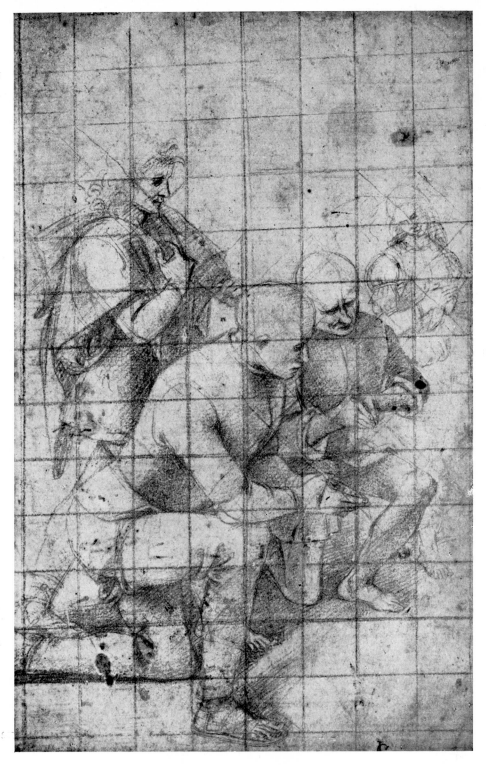

LUCA SIGNORELLI   235 *recto*

PLATE CCI

LUCA SIGNORELLI   235 *verso*

PLATE CCII

238   LUCA SIGNORELLI   234

PLATE CCIII

LUCA SIGNORELLI

237

PLATE CCIV

LUCA SIGNORELLI

PLATE CCV

LUCA SIGNORELLI

PLATE CCVI

LUCA SIGNORELLI

PLATE CCVII

LUCA SIGNORELLI 243

PLATE CCVIII

LUCA SIGNORELLI (OR AFTER)

PLATE CCIX

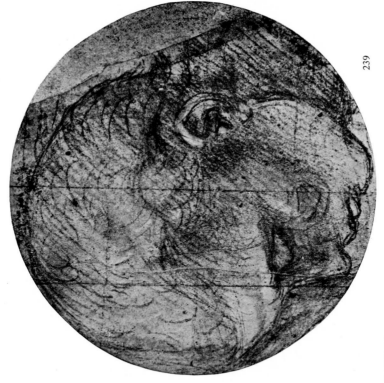

239

244

LUCA SIGNORELLI

PLATE CCX

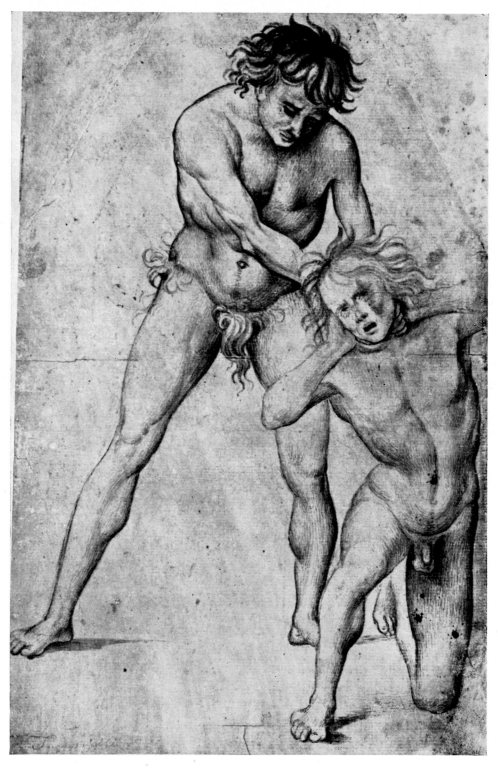

AFTER LUCA SIGNORELLI

PLATE CCXI

FOLLOWER OF LUCA SIGNORELLI   249

PLATE CCXII

LO SPAGNA

PLATE CCXIII

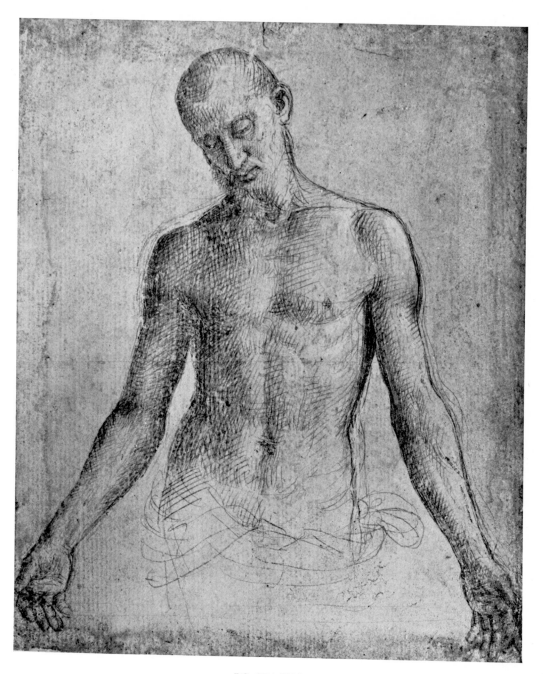

LO SPAGNA

250

PLATE CCXIV

SPERANDIO   252

STUDIO OF FRANCESCO SQUARCIONE   253

PLATE CCXV

255 *recto*

STEFANO DA VERONA   255 *verso*

PLATE CCXVI

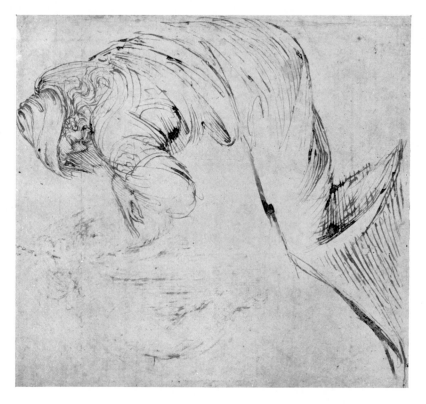

STEFANO DA VERONA

PLATE CCXVII

256

PLATE CCXVIII

ANDREA DEL VERROCCHIO   258 *recto*

PLATE CCXIX

ANDREA DEL VERROCCHIO   258 *verso*

PLATE CCXX

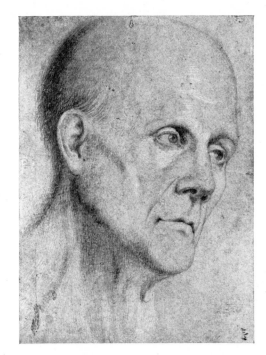

259 recto

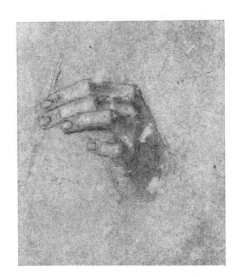

259 verso

ALVISE VIVARINI

PLATE CCXXI

IL VECCHIETTA

PLATE CCXXII

MARCO ZOPPO   260, fol. 2

PLATE CCXXIII

MARCO ZOPPO   260, fol. 7

PLATE CCXXIV

MARCO ZOPPO

PLATE CCXXV

MARCO ZOPPO   261 *recto*

PLATE CCXXVI

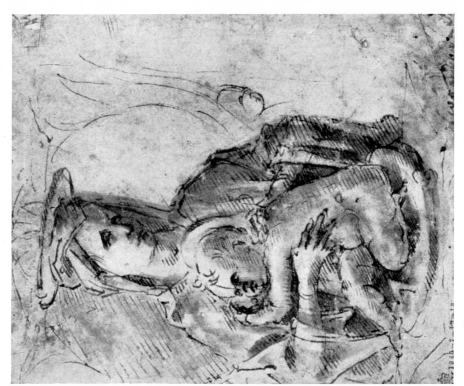

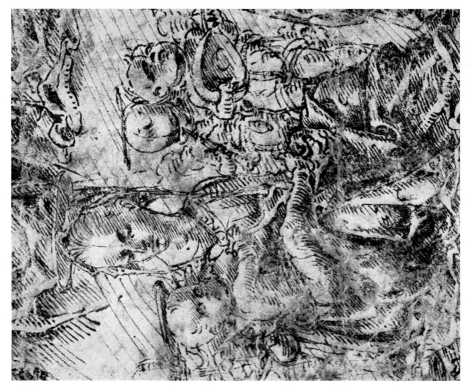

PLATE CCXXVII

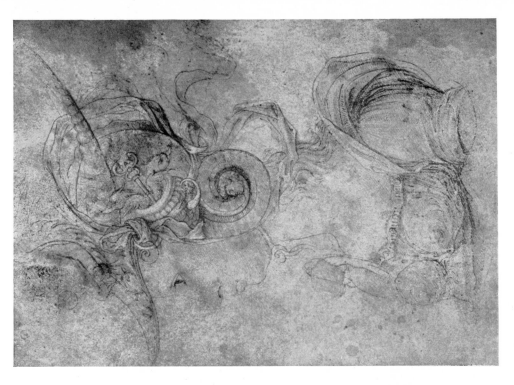

MARCO ZOPPO

263 recto

PLATE CCXXVIII

266

MARCO ZOPPO

264

PLATE CCXXIX

SIENESE (?), SECOND QUARTER OF THE FOURTEENTH CENTURY 267

PLATE CCXXX

SIENESE, THIRD QUARTER OF THE FOURTEENTH CENTURY 268

PLATE CCXXXI

SIENESE, SECOND DECADE OF THE FIFTEENTH CENTURY 270

PLATE CCXXXII

SIENESE, SECOND HALF OF THE FOURTEENTH CENTURY *269 recto*

PLATE CCXXXIII

SIENESE, SECOND HALF OF THE FOURTEENTH CENTURY   *269 verso*

PLATE CCXXXIV

271 verso

FLORENTINE, ABOUT 1400   *271 recto*

PLATE CCXXXV

TUSCAN, ABOUT 1430

PLATE CCXXXVI

273 verso

TUSCAN, ABOUT 1430

PLATE CCXXXVII

FLORENTINE, ABOUT 1460–70   274, fol. 13 *verso*

PLATE CCXXXVIII

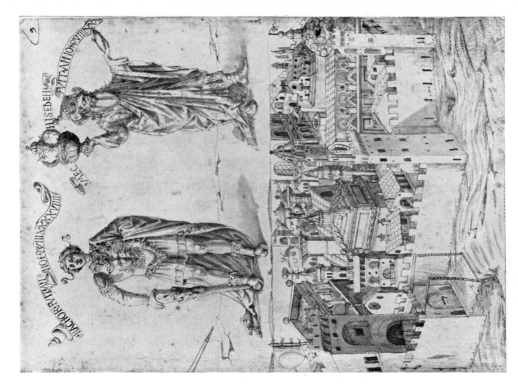

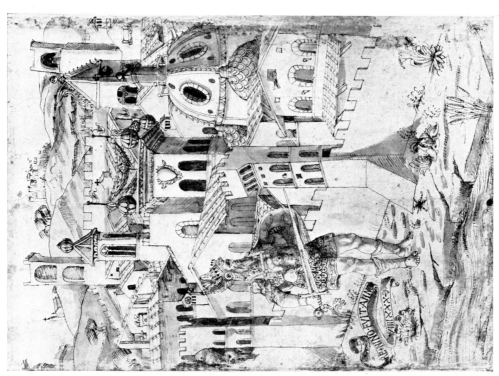

FLORENTINE, ABOUT 1460–70

PLATE CCXXXIX

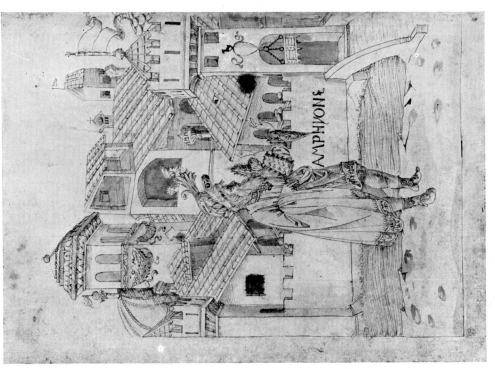

FLORENTINE, ABOUT 1460–70

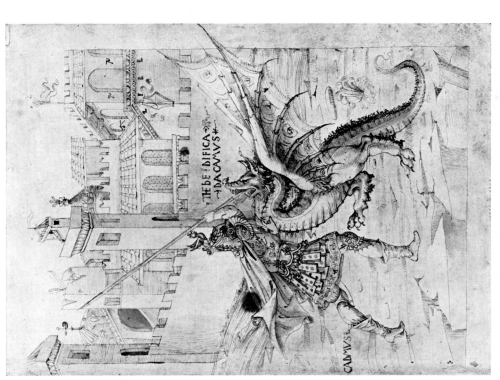

PLATE CCXL

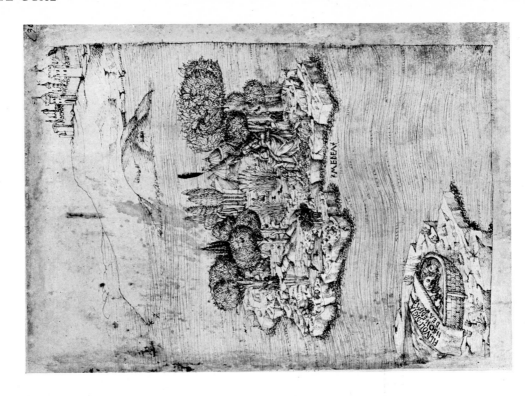

274, fol. 36 recto

FLORENTINE, ABOUT 1460–70

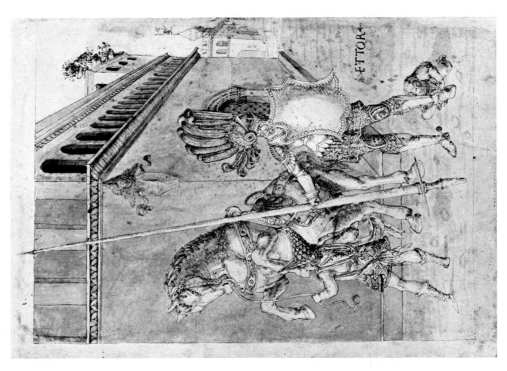

274, fol. 36 verso

PLATE CCXLI

PLATE CCXLII

FLORENTINE, THIRD QUARTER OF THE
FIFTEENTH CENTURY

276

PLATE CCXLIII

FLORENTINE, THIRD QUARTER OF THE
FIFTEENTH CENTURY

PLATE CCXLIV

FLORENTINE, ABOUT 1470

279

PLATE CCXLV

·L· PATRIARCA · AQILE·

TUSCAN (?), 1462–5 (?)   275

PLATE CCXLVI

FLORENTINE, ABOUT 1475   280

FLORENTINE (?), FIRST QUARTER OF THE FIFTEENTH CENTURY   272

PLATE CCXLVII

MARCHIGIAN (?), FIRST HALF OF THE FIFTEENTH CENTURY   282

PLATE CCXLVIII

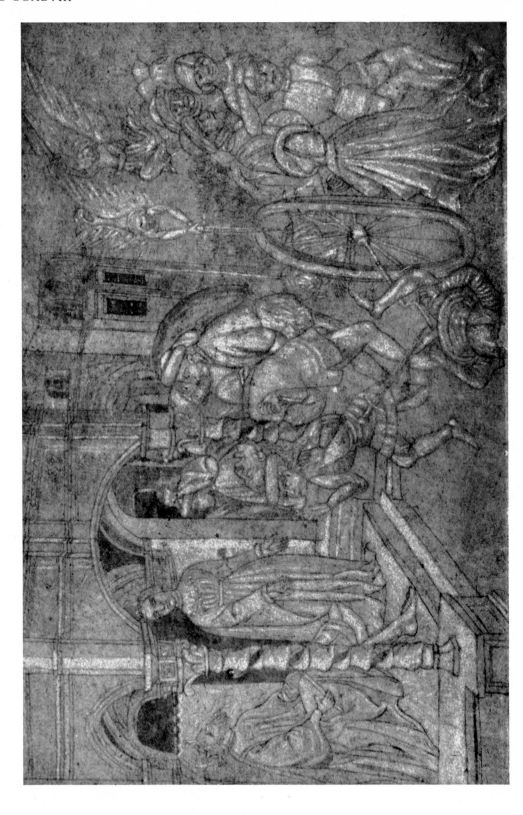

MARCHIGIAN, FIRST HALF OF THE FIFTEENTH CENTURY

PLATE CCXLIX

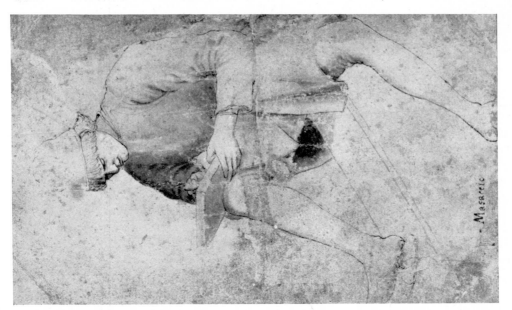

FLORENTINE, THIRD QUARTER OF THE FIFTEENTH CENTURY

PLATE CCL

EMILIAN OR LOMBARD, ABOUT 1500

286 *recto*

PLATE CCLI

EMILIAN OR LOMBARD, ABOUT 1500   *286 verso*

PLATE CCLII

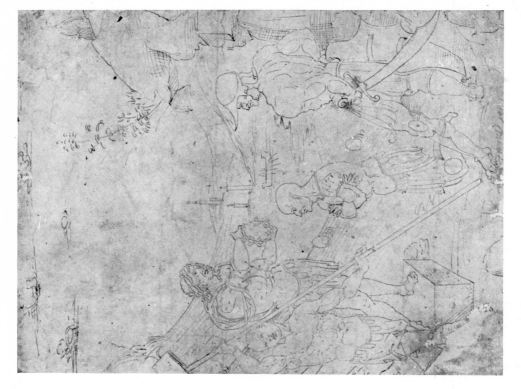

BOLOGNESE (?), ABOUT 1500

BOLOGNESE, ABOUT 1500

PLATE CCLIII

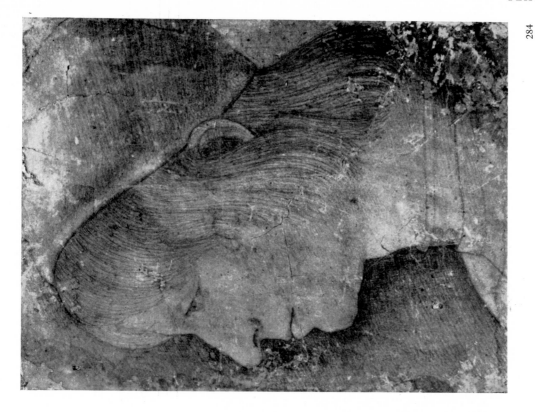

284

EMILIAN, LAST QUARTER OF THE FIFTEENTH CENTURY

281

FLORENTINE, ABOUT 1505–10

PLATE CCLIV

288

FERRARESE (?), EARLY SIXTEENTH CENTURY

PLATE CCLV

FERRARESE (?), EARLY SIXTEENTH CENTURY

PLATE CCLVI

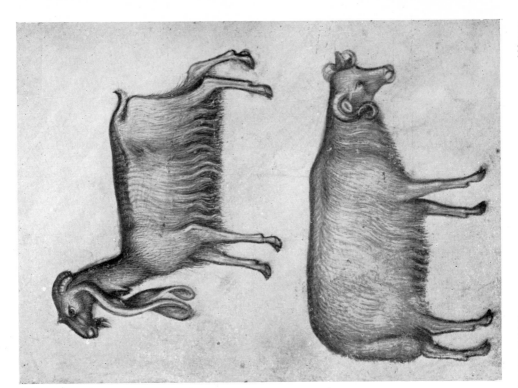

LOMBARD, ABOUT 1400

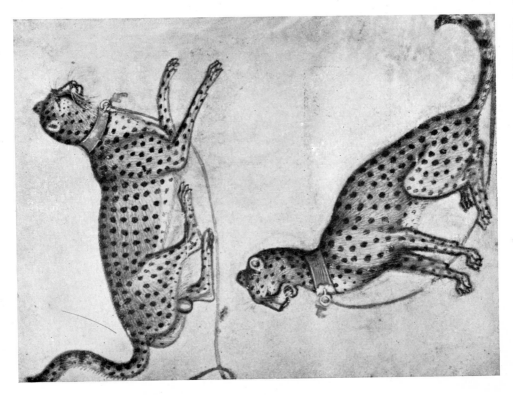

PLATE CCLVII

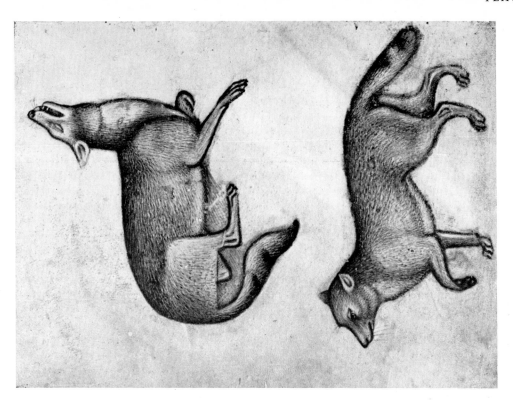

290 verso

LOMBARD, ABOUT 1400

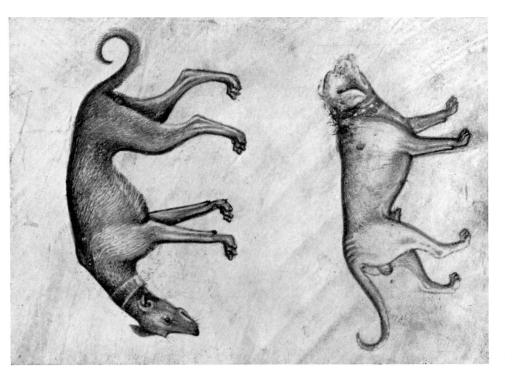

290 recto

PLATE CCLVIII

LOMBARD, ABOUT 1440–60

PLATE CCLIX

LOMBARD, ABOUT 1440–60

PLATE CCLX

MILANESE, ABOUT 1500
292
MASTER OF THE *PALA SFORZESCA*

PLATE CCLXI

LOMBARD, EARLY SIXTEENTH CENTURY   294 *recto*

PLATE CCLXII

293

MILANESE, ABOUT 1500

295

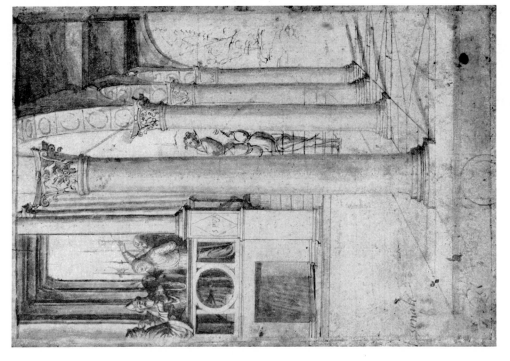

MILANESE, FIRST QUARTER OF THE SIXTEENTH
CENTURY

PLATE CCLXIII

VERONESE, FIRST HALF OF THE FIFTEENTH CENTURY

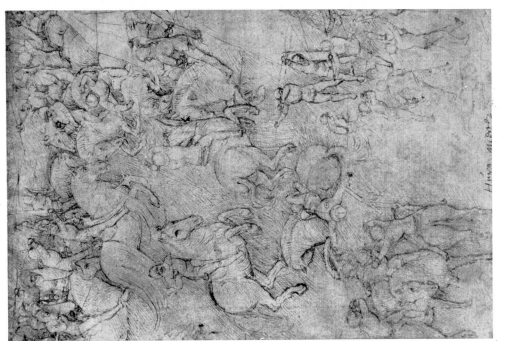

PLATE CCLXIV

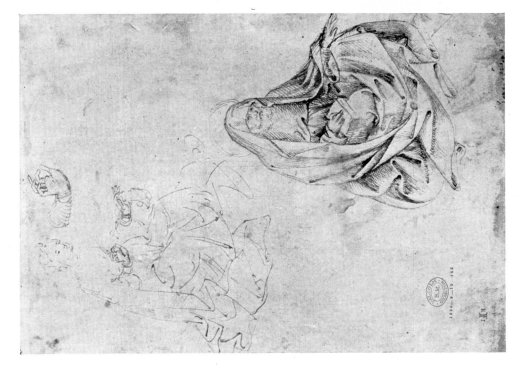

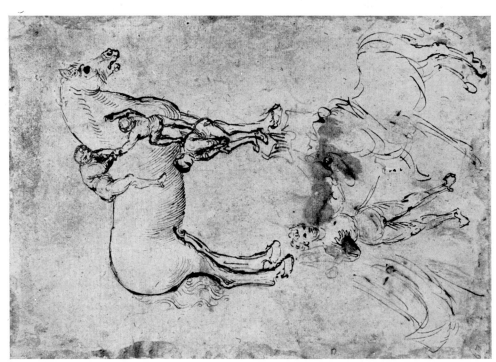

VERONESE, FIRST HALF OF THE FIFTEENTH CENTURY

PLATE CCLXV

PLATE CCLXVI

297

VERONESE, FIRST HALF OF THE FIFTEENTH CENTURY

298

PLATE CCLXVII

VERONESE, SECOND QUARTER OF THE FIFTEENTH CENTURY   302

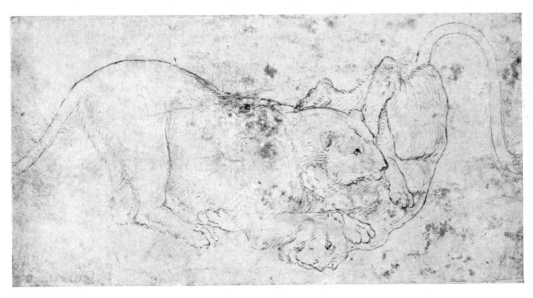

VERONESE, ABOUT 1400   296

PLATE CCLXVIII

305

VERONESE, SECOND QUARTER OF THE FIFTEENTH CENTURY

301

VERONESE, SECOND QUARTER OF THE FIFTEENTH CENTURY

PLATE CCLXIX

303

VERONESE, SECOND QUARTER OF THE FIFTEENTH CENTURY

VERONESE, EARLY SIXTEENTH CENTURY   308

PLATE CCLXX

VERONESE, ABOUT 1460

PLATE CCLXXI

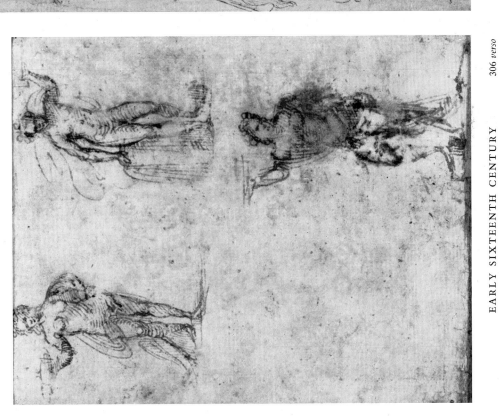

PLATE CCLXXII

PADUAN (?), LAST QUARTER OF THE FIFTEENTH CENTURY 326

PLATE CCLXXIII

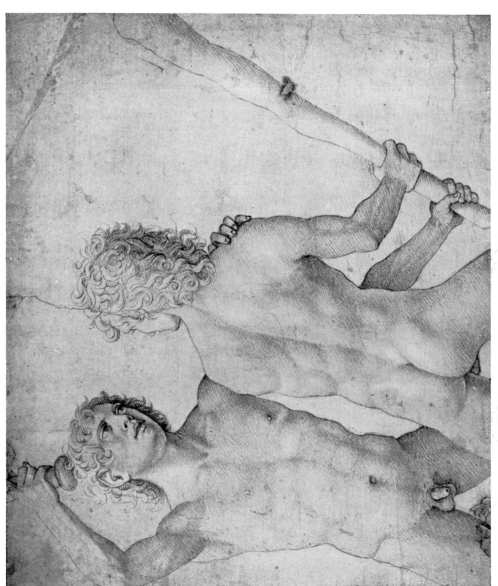

PADUAN, THIRD QUARTER OF THE FIFTEENTH CENTURY

PLATE CCLXXIV

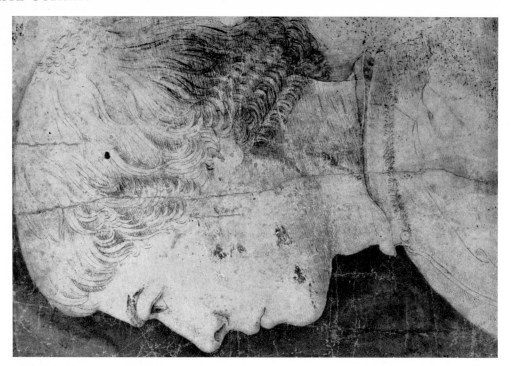

311

PADUAN, THIRD QUARTER OF THE FIFTEENTH CENTURY

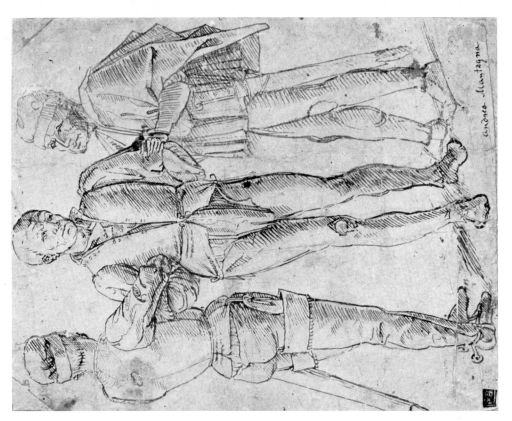

309

PADUAN, THIRD QUARTER OF THE FIFTEENTH CENTURY

PLATE CCLXXV

312

313

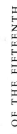

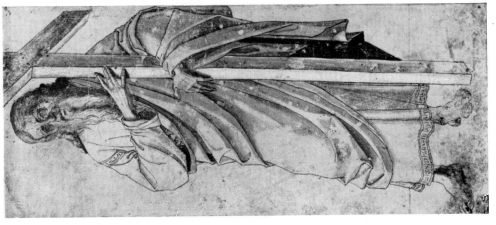

314

PADUAN (?), THIRD QUARTER OF THE FIFTEENTH CENTURY

PLATE CCLXXVI

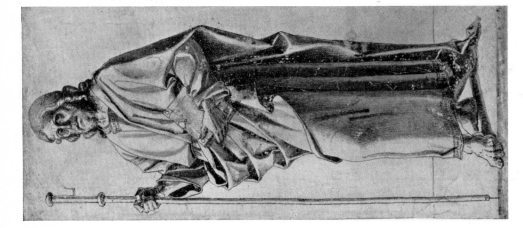

315

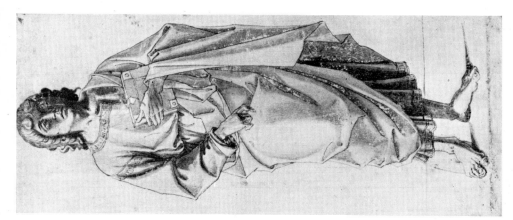

316

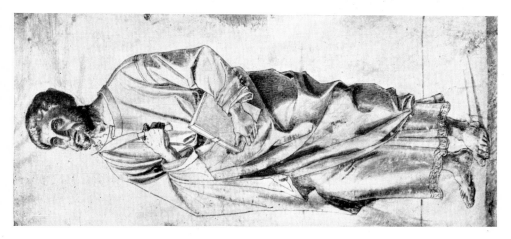

317

PADUAN (?), THIRD QUARTER OF THE FIFTEENTH CENTURY

PLATE CCLXXVII

318

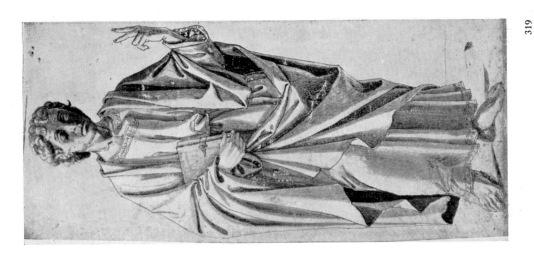

319

320

PADUAN (?), THIRD QUARTER OF THE FIFTEENTH CENTURY

PLATE CCLXXVIII

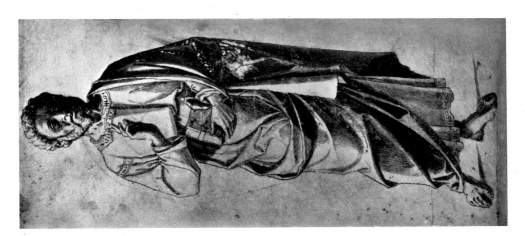

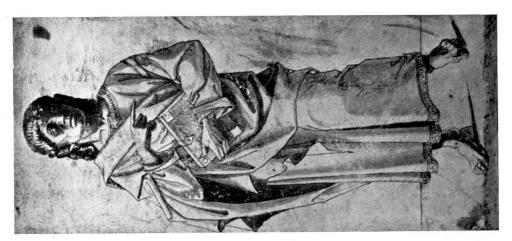

321   322   323

PADUAN (?), THIRD QUARTER OF THE FIFTEENTH CENTURY

PLATE CCLXXIX

324

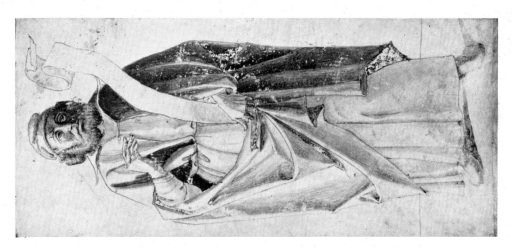

325

PADUAN (?), THIRD QUARTER OF THE FIFTEENTH CENTURY

PLATE CCLXXX

327

VENETIAN, THIRD QUARTER OF THE FIFTEENTH CENTURY

PLATE CCLXXXI

329 verso

VENETIAN, ABOUT 1500   *329 recto*

PLATE CCLXXXII

VENETIAN, LAST QUARTER OF THE FIFTEENTH CENTURY
328

PLATE CCLXXXIII

VENETIAN, ABOUT 1500

PLATE CCLXXXIV

331 *recto*

331 *verso*

NORTH ITALIAN, SECOND QUARTER OF THE FIFTEENTH CENTURY

PLATE CCLXXXV

332 recto

332 verso

NORTH ITALIAN, THIRD QUARTER OF THE FIFTEENTH
CENTURY

PLATE CCLXXXVI

333 recto

NORTH ITALIAN, ABOUT 1475

334

NORTH ITALIAN, ABOUT 1500

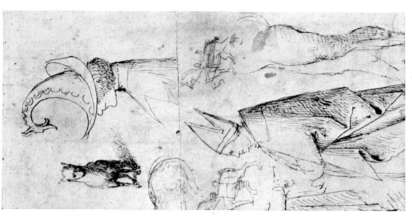

333 verso

NORTH ITALIAN, ABOUT 1475